CUSOs

CUSOs

How
CREDIT UNIONS
and
ENTREPRENEURS
Can Get Started (And Win!) with
CREDIT UNION SERVICE ORGANIZATIONS

BRIAN LAUER

LIONCREST
PUBLISHING

CUSOS

*How Credit Unions and Entrepreneurs Can Get Started
(And Win!) with Credit Union Service Organizations*

ISBN   978-1-5445-1171-9 *Paperback*

978-1-5445-1170-2 *Ebook*

To all the credit unions that strive to keep collaborating and innovating to make the financial lives of their members better. Keep moving. Keep taking risks.

And to my wife, Stacy, who makes my life better.

CONTENTS

ACKNOWLEDGMENTS

This book and its author would not be possible without some very important people in my life. First and foremost, my wife, Stacy, and my kids, Ana, Lily, and Henry, are my inspiration. They are the ones I think about when I look at myself in the mirror. My mom, Mary Beth Lauer, and my dad, George Lauer, are the reasons I was even capable of meeting someone like Stacy and raising such wonderful kids. They taught me to care about people and to endeavor to make the world a better place.

This book would also not be possible without the many ongoing conversations I've had with some very smart people who make credit unions the best financial institutions in the land. We've spent many hours over quite a few drinks strategizing the role of CUSOs as dynamic tools for achieving credit union goals. I particularly thank my law partner, Guy Messick, who took me under his wing and showed me the brilliance of working with credit unions and CUSOs. Without him, this book would surely not have been written. I also want to thank our law partner, Amanda Smith, for teaming with us in a collective commitment to our credit union and CUSO clients. This book is absolutely an offshoot of those efforts.

Many colleagues, clients, and others in the world of credit unions have influenced my career and deepened my understanding of CUSOs. Some of these enterprising people work directly with the CUSOs mentioned in these very pages. In no particular order, I call them out by name: Nick Evens, Paul Ablack, Keith Kelly, Mike Atkins, Jack Antonini, Shawna Luna, Denise Wymore, Ricky Guillot, Mark Ritter, Steve Salzer, Kirk Drake, Scott Daukas, Bruno Sementilli, Cyndie Martini, Jeff Kennedy, Jeff Russell, Kris Kovacs, Mark Zook, Vic Pantea, Deb Jones, Tina Powers, Mike Corn, Mike and Raechelle Joplin, Ben Morales, Steve McIntire, Dale Fosselman, Alessandro Pocher, Robin Kolvek, Mike Hales, Omar Jordon, Ben Rempe, Larry Jackson, Ray Crouse, Doug Peterson, Scott Jentz, Jon Jefferies, Jay Johnston, Kirk Kordeleski, Tom O'Shea, Judy Sandberg, Mary Beth Spuck, Tony Ferris, Jeff Owen, and so many more.

Let's all keep fighting the good fight.

FOREWORD

BY GUY A. MESSICK

CUSOs used to be a cute oddity, but in today's world, CUSOs have become essential to credit union sustainability. In the past ten years, the number of nonbank competitors on the internet has exploded. Superefficient, low-cost, and low-friction online services have created service expectations that seem beyond the reach of most credit unions. The cost of technology and expertise to remain competitive can be prohibitively expensive for single credit unions to afford. Adding to the woes of credit unions, the net interest spread between loans and deposits is at an all-time low. Credit unions need new answers to survive, and CUSOs provide those answers.

Our firm's involvement with the National Association of Credit Union Service Organizations, of which I've been general counsel, has placed us at the crossroads of regulators, credit unions, and innovators. We have been involved with some of the most exciting and innovative CUSOs in the country. Many of these CUSOs have made significant contributions to the success of their credit union owners and clients.

You have to see the big picture if you want to be an effective legal advisor to CUSOs. This involves seeing fine distinctions between business risks and legal risks when drawing up agreements that treat each side fairly. I've seen attorneys use "over-lawyering" tactics to position their clients in a controlling position, which only hinders the business opportunity. CUSO collaborations are not about creating winners and losers. If all parties are not in a position to mutually benefit, the collaboration will not work.

Successful CUSOs require a delicate balance of factors: vision, capable businesspeople, innovative minds, firm resolve, knowledge of the regulatory environment, deep understanding of credit union and entrepreneurial culture, and the ability to inspire, motivate, and organize people. As both a consummate businessman and talented attorney, Brian Lauer negotiates that delicate balance like no one else.

Brian has guided credit unions and innovators in creating business models that succeed and profit. He brings an entrepreneurial spirit of innovation to the business environment of CUSOs that inspires all parties in CUSO agreements. As a thought leader, he is sought after to spearhead conferences and lead discussions that expand our understanding of CUSOs in the financial marketplace.

Having spent most of my career representing credit unions and especially CUSOs, I had the good fortune more than ten years ago to bring Brian Lauer on as a partner in our firm. It was one of the best business decisions I've ever made for the clients we serve. Now that Brian has written a seminal guide to CUSOs, credit unions and entrepreneurs have the essentials at their fingertips. Brian knows the CUSO landscape from the inside out and brings it to the written page as only he can.

We're lucky to have Brian in our CUSO legal practice, and you're lucky to have his book in your hands or on your screen. I know you'll enjoy the read and learn what you need to know about the world of CUSOs.

GUY A. MESSICK

MESSICK LAUER & SMITH P.C.

INTRODUCTION

AN INSIDER'S GUIDE TO CUSOS

Credit unions are more popular than ever. Since the 2008 financial crisis, wary consumers are choosing to put their trust and banking needs in the hands of nonprofit, member-owned credit unions. These banking cooperatives provide all the financial services of community banks at significantly lower costs and higher levels of service. In today's rapidly changing financial marketplace, credit unions are increasingly significant players.

Credit unions are adept at meeting consumer needs. Yet as nonprofit organizations, they have needs of their own. In particular, credit unions need to maximize efficiencies in order to flourish. One way they do this is by joining together in collaborative organizations called Credit Union Service Organizations, or CUSOs for short.

CUSOs have the collective ability to lower the costs of the financial services they offer their members.

For example, business loan underwriting can require a great deal of expertise. Smaller credit unions typically don't have that kind of expertise on staff. The solution is to come together in a CUSO to pool their resources. In this way, they can gain access to a broader base of talent and share the cost of that talent to serve more of their members' needs.

CUSOs therefore help individual credit unions expand services by increasing efficiencies through economies of scale. When credit unions cooperate and innovate through CUSOs, they generate additional income, tap into greater expertise, develop new inventive ideas, and reduce spending. It's a win for credit unions.

A VISION SHARED

At my law firm, we've been helping credit unions join together in CUSOs for more than thirty years, and we've seen positive results for both credit unions and their members. Individual credit unions are successfully driving down their operating expenses and thriving.

Every financial institution has burdens that must be addressed, from regulatory compliance to cybersecurity.

Technology-based requirements are expensive when done individually. But when credit unions consolidate their back offices and information technology cooperatively through CUSOs, they lower operating expenses and save their credit unions tons of money. CUSOs allow credit unions to be nimbler and save on IT vendor costs through their collective buying power.

For instance, after a business loan is originated by a credit union, its CUSO takes over and handles the more expensive back-office operations. Both underwriting and servicing for the loans are handled by the CUSO. This significantly drives down the individual credit union's service costs. The CUSO gives the credit union the power to "outsource" its business loans to its own larger organization.

WHY CUSOS NOW?

Today, we see a lot of movement and innovation in the financial services sector. At the same time, credit unions are generating more income by expanding their services and financial horizons.

Credit unions have traditionally followed a classic lending model. Until about twenty-five years ago, a credit union could survive with the basics. They took deposits from credit union members, paid interest on those deposits, and used those funds to make home, auto, and small business loans to their members. There was a great yield spread in the credit union model; operating expenses were much lower than interest rates. The regulatory burden and technology costs were also lower. It was just simpler to run a credit union back then.

But times have changed. With the evolving complexities of financial services, credit union operating expenses have grown. As online and alternative lenders have entered the financial services marketplace, credit unions today face more competition for loans. It used to be that when a credit union member needed a car loan or a mortgage loan, they'd get it directly from the credit union without question. Now, they're more likely to shop around online and get quotes from different lenders. Even Costco is in the car loan business. As competition has grown and as consumers demand convenient access to more financial services, credit unions have had to adapt.

By forming and investing in CUSOs, credit unions have empowered themselves and their members in a new strategic vision. CUSOs have become more significant players in the industry. By entering new markets, credit unions can provide the services their members need. By working together in collaborative CUSOs, credit unions have found the twenty-first-century key to profitability.

OPPORTUNITIES FOR INNOVATION

A credit union is a trusted advisor to its members. It sees itself as an important part of its members' lives, and it wants to stay relevant and useful. In an increasingly competitive market, credit unions want to be part of their members' financial life. And through their collaboration in CUSOs, credit unions have gained greater access to service and growth opportunities.

To stay competitive, credit unions, like other financial institutions, are looking toward innovation in financial services. They are partnering with entrepreneurs to develop new technologies, such as unique lending platforms and loan application processes that provide members the convenient access to services they desire. A credit union that can make a loan decision in only minutes is way ahead of the game.

Credit unions are sometimes relatively large organizations, yet they are nonprofits that run like smaller institutions. Their focus is on what's good for their members. Credit unions are more accessible and therefore more attractive to tech entrepreneurs than multinational banks such as Chase, Wells Fargo, or Bank of America. Credit unions are people oriented and more willing to talk, offering easier access to partnering opportunities, capital for development costs, and the ability to get products to market more quickly. Therefore, entrepreneurs and service providers are more inclined to work with credit unions to create innovative solutions. Also, as we'll see in later chapters, it's common for tech entrepreneurs to partner with credit unions in CUSOs.

YOUR INSIDER'S GUIDE

As you've seen, CUSOs present distinct advantages to credit unions. They generate greater interest income, as well as noninterest income, while providing expanded services to their members. They provide access to higher levels of expertise and wider fields of organizational talent, while driving down operating expenses. And they provide for levels of innovation and competitiveness necessary in an ever-evolving, digitized financial services sector. But this is just the short list.

In the following pages, you'll gain an insider's view of how credit unions, entrepreneurs, and service providers are making the most of CUSOs. You'll learn the ins and outs and varied ways in which CUSOs can meet your professional and organizational needs.

I'll show you the lay of the land in the regulatory realm and the particulars of forming a CUSO. Sometimes forming and using CUSOs can be difficult. I will give some insights into how to form successful CUSOs. Along the way, you'll see why service providers and entrepreneurs are increasingly looking to CUSOs as innovative business incubators. So, let's get started.

CHAPTER ONE

UNDERSTANDING THE WORLD OF CREDIT UNIONS

As nonprofit financial organizations, credit unions exist to serve their members. Lower costs and higher levels of service are baked into their DNA. Credit unions are increasingly providing a broader range of financial services, and CUSOs are helping them do it. But before we go more deeply into CUSOs, let's have a look at the financial and human nature of credit unions.

A COMMON BOND

Credit unions came about to fill a need. The earliest credit unions in America were founded to help farmers and others in underserved communities get access to affordable loans. Early credit unions were sometimes called people's banks. They gained popularity as an honest alternative to profit-driven banks that charged excessive fees or were quick to repossess property, such as financially strapped farms.

It's no wonder that credit unions have flourished and grown to serve more than 102 million members today. Nearly one-third of the US population are account holders in federally chartered credit unions. This should give credit unions considerable leverage in the financial system, and by coming together as CUSOs, they are better able to use that leverage.

Federally chartered credit unions are granted a field of membership by the National Credit Union Administration (NCUA), a government body. They can also be chartered by individual states. The definition of what constitutes a credit union's "field of membership" and the nature of restrictions in charters are very significant factors in the formation and operation of credit unions.

A credit union's field of membership is determined by the type of "common bond" among its members, such as geography, trade, industry, or profession. Members can have a single common bond, such as a shared community, or multiple common bonds, such as a community, an occupation, or an employer. Broadening the definition of common bonds can make it easier for credit unions to charter, compete, and thrive.

When a credit union forms, it chooses its field of membership. Federally chartered credit unions can charter in one of three ways. The first way is a single associational or common bond. This can be a trade group, an employee group, or another single common bond. A second way to charter is in a multiple common bond. Here, the field of membership is broader and can include more than one trade group, employee group, or association. A third way is a community charter, which is relatively new for federally chartered credit unions. It allows a credit union to serve a particular geographic community. This is how it works at the federal level, but for states, it's a different ball game.

At the state level, regulators in a particular state set their own field-of-membership rules. State charters tend to be broader and more liberal than federal charters. In some states, credit unions don't have to choose between a single common bond or a community bond. Those states allow an employee group and a community to come together under the same charter. Some states also allow for very broad definitions of community that can extend the field of membership to the entire state, including anyone who lives, works, or worships in that state. Some credit unions have therefore been converting exclusively to state charters in order to make it easier to grow and expand membership.

Credit union members typically live in the same community, work for the same company, or have other professional or community connections. Their membership in the credit union brings them together in collective ownership. It gives them a shared stake in a financial institution, similar in some ways to shareholders of for-profit banks. However, there are big differences.

Commercial and community banks are usually owned by a handful of people who hold all the shares and make all the decisions. These stakeholders want a return on their investment, so they encourage financial activity that drives profit. It's the classic example of a select few making money off the community.

Credit unions are nonprofits based on a completely different cooperative model. They aren't driven by profit motive but rather by a model of service to their members. All members are coequal, and each has the same stake no matter how much money they have on deposit or how many financial services they use. Each member has one vote in electing a board of directors to provide oversight.

This isn't to say that credit unions don't need to generate profits. The pressures on credit unions from competing financial institutions require that they find ways of generating income and driving down operating expenses. The difference is that credit union profits are used to sustain the organization, not to pay a return on investment to individuals and put money in anyone's pockets. Any profit on a credit union's books is used to either shore up its reserves against loan losses or to shore up its capital position for future expenditures on member services. A credit union's profit goes to sustaining the organization. If a credit union does distribute its profit, they go to all members and not a select few.

In contrast to for-profit banks that make money by charging various fees to customers, credit unions strive to reduce fees and interest rates paid on traditional financial services. The financial philosophy of credit unions is to create benefits for their membership communities. Financial literacy and education are part of the services they provide. This cooperative model helps establish credit unions as trusted financial advisors to their members with their best interests at heart.

GETTING CREDIT UNIONS INSURED

At the beginning of the Great Depression when financial markets tanked and a third of banks failed, depositors lost their life savings. Those were the rough-and-tumble days of runs on banks when people were desperate to make withdrawals before their banks went under. To restore confidence in the American banking system, the Federal Deposit Insurance Corporation (FDIC) was formed in 1933 to insure accounts up to $2,500. This figure has risen over the years, and in 2008, in reaction to the financial crisis, the insured amount was increased to $250,000.

However, FDIC protections don't extend to credit union deposits. Credit unions are in a unique category, and here's why: credit union members aren't just depositors. Technically, they're shareholders, so since 1970, their savings have been insured by the National Credit Union Share Insurance Fund (NCUSIF), not the FDIC. Some $1 trillion in member shares are insured up to $250,000 per share by the "full faith and credit" of the US government.

Every federally chartered credit union is required to have share insurance, while state-chartered credit unions are required by their states to also carry federal share insurance, or, as in some states, alternative private share insurance instead.

When the NCUA audits a federal credit union, they examine not only the credit union's operations, but their financial safety and soundness. It isn't so much that they're looking out for members; it's more that they want to make sure nothing will jeopardize the share insurance fund. For state-chartered credit unions, state regulators examine operations and the NCUA looks out for safety and soundness. This dual nature of regulations creates a unique legal area in which state-chartered credit unions are sometimes subject to federal regulations and sometimes to state regulations.

LEVELING THE FINANCIAL FIELD

The traditional model for banking has always been that profit is driven purely by making loans at a certain interest rate and taking deposits at a lower interest rate. Profit is in the difference between the two. For decades, credit unions survived by following this time-honored model. They've made loans and received deposits, making sure there was a yield spread between the interest rates for loans and the deposit rates they gave members on their share accounts.

Over the last fifteen to twenty years, however, this model has dried up. Pressures in the market have changed the financial landscape and made the traditional model obsolete. Over the past two decades, operating expenses have gone through the roof due to escalating costs of compliance and technology. It's costing more and more to provide even the simplest, bare-bones financial services. Higher levels of skills are required to navigate the changes, and specialized staff cost more, too. At the same time, interest rates have gone down to the point that operating expenses have surpassed interest income.

Credit unions can no longer exist on the old model. This

is why the number of credit unions has been shrinking at the rate of about one a day for the past twenty years. Sometimes they liquidate or are liquidated by regulators for case-by-case reasons, but for the most part, they've been merging with other credit unions. Small credit unions just don't have the scale to survive, so they merge with larger credit unions or go under.

Like any business, a credit union needs to maximize efficiencies in order to flourish. But credit unions have special considerations for investing in outside companies. Everything must go back into the organization. This is the unique nature of credit unions. They are chartered and regulated at the federal or state level according to strict parameters that can sometimes hamstring their opportunities for investment in broader for-profit markets.

This is where CUSOs provide an advantage. When credit unions join together in CUSOs, they gain the collective ability to lower costs for their financial services. Because CUSOs aren't governed by the same tight regulations as individual credit unions, they can provide credit unions with the access they need to wider investment markets. CUSOs therefore open doors for investment and financial innovation opportunities that credit unions wouldn't otherwise have.

For credit unions trying to survive, CUSOs level the financial playing field. CUSOs put credit unions in a position to generate additional interest income that improves on the traditional model. CUSOs can also go further by opening access to noninterest income, such as insurance services and investment and financial advisory services.

In this new model, credit unions can also provide services to other credit unions, such as mortgage lending. By allowing for collaboration among credit unions, CUSOs drive down operating costs and get better scale for operational services. Instead of a credit union having to merge with another credit union, it can reduce its costs and operating expenses by collaborating in a CUSO. In this way, credit unions team together to jointly provide back-office services such as loan origination or financial software.

CUSOs allow nonprofit credit unions to invest in for-profit entities that generate income for their balance sheets. This ability to invest in more dynamic models stimulates earnings that afford better services to credit union members. In this way, CUSOs help credit unions compete with for-profit financial institutions on more equal footing.

CREDIT UNIONS TODAY

As membership-based financial organizations, credit unions continue to fill a vital function. In our competitive society and expanding global marketplace, the cooperative model allows individuals and communities fair access to financial services. Credit unions ensure that everyday people are protected and not oversold on financial products and services they may or may not need.

When we hear news reports about financial institutions such as Wells Fargo overselling and cross-selling products, we are reminded of the financial crisis of 2008 and the ballooning mortgages that were sold to unsuspecting home buyers. Credit unions are the opposite of self-serving banks and lenders. Credit unions were formed for the express purpose of providing American farmers, families, and aspiring business owners the loans they needed to realize their dreams or to simply stay afloat until harvest time or through hard financial times.

Credit unions today continue to advance individuals and communities, rolling out new financial products and services aimed at helping the underserved consumer. Credit unions are middle-class institutions focused exclusively on serving their members and promoting their financial interests in an increasingly competitive marketplace.

In the next chapter, we'll take a closer look at how credit unions are innovating and expanding their influence through CUSOs.

CHAPTER TWO

HOW CUSOS BENEFIT CREDIT UNIONS

CUSOs benefit credit unions by helping credit unions to expand services and increase efficiencies through economies of scale. In an ever more competitive financial marketplace, CUSOs are helping to level the playing field by giving credit unions a leg up to the competition. CUSOs aren't governed by the same regulations as individual credit unions, so they offer credit unions access to a wider market of products and services.

In this chapter, we'll take a deeper dive into the ways in which CUSOs benefit credit unions.

BENEFITS OF CUSOS

There are four major reasons why credit unions actively

seek to align themselves with CUSOs; each yields clear benefits to individual credit unions. These are income, expertise, innovation, and savings.

1. INCOME

Financial institutions used to flourish by making more in interest on loans than on the interest rates they paid to their depositors. However, as we saw in Chapter One, the traditional business model is no longer working. In our ever-expanding financial marketplace, the costs to credit unions for basic financial services, including compliance, technology, and specialized staff have driven up operating expenses. Credit unions have therefore had to adapt to survive, and they've done this by finding opportunities to generate additional sources of income through CUSOs.

In this new model, there are basically two kinds of income available to credit unions: interest income and noninterest income.

Interest Income

Interest income is the traditional model, but now with an added twist. Credit unions traditionally made consumer loans, such as auto loans or unsecured signature loans for personal expenses, like Christmas loans. By partnering in CUSOs, credit unions can now extend their capacity to make more loans.

For example, a credit union that has traditionally made auto loans can partner with a CUSO that has wider access to auto dealerships. The credit union can now expand its auto loan volume by participating in an auto lending CUSO. In this model, it's the dealer who actually initiates and makes the loan, then the credit union buys it from them. But in order to do this, the credit union needs to have a relationship with the dealer, and that relationship comes through the CUSO.

CU Direct is a CUSO in the auto loan sphere that has been in business since the 1980s. One of the earliest and largest CUSOs, CU Direct started as a way for credit unions to get access to auto lending opportunities and interest income. Credit unions historically got their start in consumer loans, and by the 1960s were doing a lot of business in auto loans. However, their market for auto loans began to shrink as auto dealers themselves began originating on-the-spot loans for car buyers. The dealers would then assign that financing to a lender. What CU Direct did was to create its own network with auto dealers to assign those loans to credit union lenders. Through CU Direct, credit unions get access to the dealer network, which is a conduit between dealers and credit unions. The network operates via software that originates and processes credit union loans directly at the auto dealers' offices. The result has been more auto loans and interest income for credit unions.

CUSOs are also providing credit unions with the ability to expand their lending into the broader market of business and commercial loans. CUSOs offer the expertise credit unions need in commercial loan underwriting, processing, and servicing to book business loans. This is opening new opportunities for interest income on commercial lending that credit unions didn't have before.

An example of a business lending CUSO is Member Business Financial Services (MBFS) LLC, originally formed by seven credit unions in eastern Pennsylvania. On their own, none of the credit unions had been able to offer their members business loans. So they decided to come together to form a CUSO and hired a specialized staff to originate, underwrite, and service business loans. Over time, MBFS merged with another CUSO doing exactly the same thing in western Pennsylvania, and together they expanded to serve credit unions across the entire state of Pennsylvania.

Noninterest Income

Noninterest income is earned on fees charged for products and services. Credit unions are traditionally community oriented and exist to provide their members with cost-effective financial products and services. Therefore, they're not looking to generate noninterest income by charging fees. Instead, they look to CUSOs to provide access to financial services that members would traditionally find elsewhere.

The perfect example of this is insurance. A credit union can form a CUSO that is set up as its own insurance agency. The CUSO can sell property insurance, casualty insurance, homeowners, auto, and umbrella insurance to their members. The CUSO receives the customary commission typically generated on policies sold through an insurance carrier. The commissions are built into the cost of insurance. They aren't the typically punitive, arbitrary charges for insufficient balance payments or bounced checks fees.

In addition to generating additional noninterest income from a credit union's members, CUSOs, unlike credit unions, are permitted to serve people who are not credit union members. Therefore, by serving nonmembers, CUSOs can open doors to new revenue streams and broaden the market for credit unions to generate income.

An example of a CUSO that earns noninterest income is CUSO Financial Services (CFS). CFS is one of the premier broker-dealers serving the credit union marketplace. It had its inception when several vendors in the financial services industry realized that most broker-dealer arrangements weren't cost-effective for credit unions. They reached out to several credit union leaders who agreed and formed CFS as a broker-dealer company. CFS is owned by its credit union founders and operated by the vendors who helped conceive it. Over ten years or so, CFS has generated more than $50 million in dividends for its equity owners. It serves the broader credit union community that uses CFS's financial services as clients.

2. EXPERTISE

When a credit union works with a CUSO to expand its service offerings into the broader market, the credit union benefits from the CUSO's expertise. Several credit unions that want to offer new services could come together to form a CUSO to provide that service. This is both highly efficient and effective because it leads to superior expertise shared by several credit unions. There's power in numbers. As a collaboration of several credit unions, the CUSO can share expenses to hire the best employees for a fraction of the cost.

The CUSO can also provide those services to other credit unions that are not part of the collaborative CUSO. This increases the earning power of the credit unions that formed the CUSO. Now that they are up and operating, they can use their excess capacity to serve other credit unions and collect the fees. A single, highly expert and shared department can serve a credit union much more efficiently than a small department contained within one credit union. It affords the hiring of talented people who can drive income for the participating credit unions.

For example, a dozen or so credit unions came together in the southwest United States, forming a CUSO called Credit Union Financial Network (CUFN), to manage securities investment for their members. Investment services require expertise and specialized skills to manage relationships with Securities and Exchange Commission (SEC)-licensed brokers, dealers, and registered representatives who sell securities. Some credit unions can do this on their own, but others don't have the skills on staff. CUFN provides the service and assists credit unions in generating income. Financial services CUSOs of this type also exist in the investment, commercial lending, and mortgage arenas, as well as in the indirect lending space.

Another example of using collaboration to maximize expertise and minimize costs is Business Alliance Financial Services (BAFS) in Louisiana. BAFS is a business lending CUSO that helps credit unions pool their resources so that each doesn't have to support its own commercial lending department. Eleven credit unions support one business lending department that provides superior underwriting and loan processing expertise. BAFS brings together a great deal of knowledge and experience in providing US Department of Agriculture loans prevalent in that region of the country. They bring a high level of service to their rural community membership in Louisiana and parts of Arkansas and Texas. BAFS does all the underwriting, analysis, and processing of loans for its credit union partners and other credit unions who participate as clients.

Commercial lending CUSOs, such as BAFS, build a network of trust among participating credit unions that makes it possible for credit unions to sell loans or pieces of loans to other credit unions. This helps credit unions spread their risk. Consider the example of a small rural credit union that has an opportunity to make a $5 million loan that would be great for their community, but they don't have the funds to do it. A commercial lending CUSO can provide the expertise to underwrite and analyze a loan of that size and caliber. It can also provide a network of participating credit unions that can collaborate to hold a piece of the loan. In this way, smaller credit unions can better serve their communities while sharing loan ownership, risk, and income.

3. INNOVATION

Service delivery channels are extremely important to the credit union industry. These include everything from payment services and remote check deposit services to online banking. These digital platforms are always evolving with more efficient and innovative technologies. So there's a constant stream of innovation in software products for generating and modifying loans and better ways to provide mobile and online access to financial products and services. CUSOs are helping credit unions access these new delivery channels and are opening doors for credit unions to invest in new financial products.

To do this, CUSOs partner with technology entrepreneurs to develop innovative financial technologies, often called fintech. These are typically startup companies that develop products and services, such as lending platforms and loan application processes. The startups that develop these products need access to financial institutions and their customers. They also need certain required licenses and authorizations. CUSOs have the licenses, or aren't required to have them, so they are attractive business partners for tech entrepreneurs. They are also more accessible than global banks, so tech entrepreneurs seek partnerships with credit unions. At the same time, fintech entrepreneurs are frequently looking for investors. They need development money and strategic partners.

For credit unions, it's an opportunity to earn income on a good investment. By investing in fintech through CUSOs, they gain a stake in a third-party company that's providing a product to their members. This kind of strategic investment comes with a degree of control over delivery channels. In this way, a credit union becomes both a customer and a stakeholder with more influence over the strategic vision of a new service platform. It's a win-win scenario for credit unions, which are member-driven organizations with a service-oriented philosophy.

An example of this kind of tech innovation in member services is CU Realty Services, which is a CUSO partnership of credit unions and the real estate industry. CU Realty Services provides specialized internal software that gives credit union members access to multiple listing services for homes. These home listing services are an inside track to home buying and selling. The partnership also provides members with access to affiliated real estate agents and brokers to help them in the buying and selling process. The arrangement operates as an affinity program offering buyers and sellers rebates of 20 percent on real estate commissions. The program is available in states where regulations permit such discounts. It's a boon to credit unions, because members who use the service are more likely to apply for a mortgage through their credit union, though they aren't required to do so. The service deepens the relationship of trust and affinity between credit unions and their members.

4. SAVINGS

The fourth reason credit unions actively seek to align themselves with CUSOs is savings. CUSOs provide credit unions with tangible cost savings through economy of scale. As we discussed in Chapter One, credit union operating expenses keep going up, while income in the traditional model keeps going down. But when credit unions come together collaboratively in CUSOs, they can consolidate shared services more economically.

An example of this is the use of core processing systems. Core processors are essential for the full range of financial accounting; they are the backbone of the entire operation and are very expensive to purchase, run, and maintain. Yet when several credit unions join together to form a CUSO, they are able to share the expense of core processing. They essentially have one IT department running the core processing system.

This results in big savings for the credit unions involved. They have better aggregate buying power to negotiate for additional products and services as well. Through their association in a CUSO, they are seen as a much larger institution in the marketplace and reap the savings.

For example, consider a CUSO formed by Franklin Mint Federal Credit Union in the Philadelphia area. The credit union found that it had become too costly to maintain their own mortgage department and all the incurred expenses of software, services, and staff. What they decided to do was move their mortgage department into a CUSO called State Financial Network and sell those mortgage services to other credit unions as well, which made the operation more economical.

By moving their mortgage operation into a CUSO and providing those services to other credit unions, they could offset the cost of providing mortgage services to their own members. Also, by increasing their volume, they were able to get better pricing on the sale of their mortgages on the secondary market. Basically, they took the fixed cost of providing mortgage services to their own members and leveraged it into a CUSO that saved money by providing those services to other credit unions as well.

In a similar vein, some credit unions have moved their indirect lending resources into CUSOs. Lending resources, such as auto dealer networks, have maintenance costs. By forming an indirect lending CUSO and opening their dealer network to other credit unions, a credit union can offset their costs and reap savings.

STAYING ALIVE

In addition to the four reasons just discussed—income, expertise, innovation, and savings—there's one more reason credit unions align themselves with CUSOs. And the reason is simple: staying alive.

As we've seen, credit unions trying to survive have had to improve on the traditional banking model. CUSOs open doors to credit unions for opportunities to invest in more dynamic financial models that stimulate earnings. In this way, CUSOs help credit unions compete with for-profit financial institutions on more equal footing. By aligning in CUSOs, credit unions can offer their members more services while increasing income and maintaining their independence.

Two of the oldest and largest CUSOs in the industry are CO-OP Financial Services in California and PSCU in Florida. Both were early players in providing credit unions with access to products and services that helped credit unions compete in the changing financial services marketplace.

CO-OP started as a partnership of credit unions that weren't large enough on their own to gain access to automated teller machines. As a new customer convenience, ATMs were all the rage in the early 1980s, and credit unions needed to get on board. CO-OP offered credit unions their own ATM network, which started in 1981 with twenty ATMs. Over the years, CO-OP has grown in products and services to include processing and payment tools, consulting, and shared branching networks, along with upward of 30,000 surcharge-free ATMs.

PSCU began in the late 1970s with a mission of providing credit unions with sorely needed access to credit card networks. What began as a partnership of five credit unions quickly grew to thirty-six within one year, and to 275 credit unions five years later. By 1991, PSCU was also servicing debit card programs. During their long history, PSCU has provided credit unions with early access to leading-edge financial technologies, including data analytics, digital payments, call center support, and digital wallets. They are a quintessential example of a well-connected industry player that gives credit unions a competitive edge to compete in the evolving financial landscape.

CUSOs such as CO-OP and PSCU are driving down operating costs and helping credit unions increase their income, which is a powerful combination. In this way, CUSOs continue to accelerate the growth of credit unions through a financial technology infrastructure and services.

CUSOS AT WORK

Not only do CUSOs provide for the specific needs of credit unions, but they also are often very interesting enterprises in and of themselves. One such CUSO goes by the name of Ongoing Operations. It was formed as a collaborative of several credit unions to provide financial disaster recovery services.

The concept for Ongoing Operations came about as a result of the 9/11 attacks on the World Trade Center in New York's financial district and the Pentagon in 2001. The credit unions that formed Ongoing Operations are located in Washington, DC, where the Pentagon was attacked and anthrax bacteria scares occurred in the weeks after. Financial institutions in New York were deeply affected by 9/11, and law enforcement had to shut down parts of America's capital city.

In the aftermath, these credit unions in DC realized that as financial institutions, they didn't have the right recovery operations. On their own, they didn't possess the expertise for software systems recovery and business continuity. They lacked the policies and procedures necessary to continue to provide services to their members in the event of a disaster. Rather than seek expensive outside vendors, they decided to come together to form a company and hire the recovery experts for themselves. They established a cost-effective alternative that has evolved into a company that serves credit unions nationwide and has expanded into cloud computing services.

Ongoing Operations is a real-world example of how CUSOs benefit credit unions in the areas of fintech investment, innovation, expertise, and savings. It shows how CUSOs open doors to investment and financial opportunities that credit unions wouldn't otherwise have.

CHAPTER THREE

CUSOS AND COLLABORATION

As we've seen, credit unions came into being as cooperative organizations to solve a problem. The problem was that many individuals and families in communities across the nation lacked access to banking services, primarily credit services. Credit unions formed as collectives of people coming together to help each other gain access to credit. Over time, however, economic stress has disrupted the credit union business model. Increased competition and compliance costs, operating expenses, labor costs, and IT costs have exerted downward pressure on credit unions.

The good news is that the same kind of cooperative spirit that generated credit unions in the first place contributes to the formation of CUSOs. CUSOs are a new kind of collaboration comprised of credit unions coming together to solve shared problems. CUSOs are therefore cooperatives of cooperatives. In the CUSO business model, individual credit unions partner together to pool resources in new collaborative enterprises that benefit all members.

An example of this collaboration is Currencé, a CUSO partnership of six credit unions that share negotiating power in the Visa credit and debit card market. Currencé was initially founded by credit unions to receive better rates from Visa. As small credit unions, each individually didn't have the clout to access one of the premier providers in the credit and debit card market. By joining together, they could negotiate and contract with Visa as one entity through the CUSO. Currencé does all the administration, while the processing itself is done through Visa. The company also serves other credit union clients who benefit through the access Currencé provides.

WHY COLLABORATE?

One of the primary downward pressures on credit unions has been increased operating expenses. It has become imperative for credit unions to limit operating expenses in order to serve their members without increasing costs. Credit unions have realized that administrative costs can be reduced through collaboration in the form of CUSOs. The guiding principle is that collaboration creates scale.

Scale in business is about growing revenue while limiting

operating costs. When credit unions come together to collaborate in CUSOs, they are partnering to increase their scale. Like any company, when a credit union scales its business, it optimizes resources while lowering its expenses. So when we talk about CUSOs and collaboration, what we're really talking about is credit unions coming together to share in the cost of operating expenses. In this way, they scale their operations for increased purchasing power for the benefit of their members.

An example of collaboration to gain value from scale is a CUSO called Member Loyalty Group. It was formed to give credit unions access to specialized member survey services. Several credit unions came together to negotiate the use of survey software called Satmetrix. It's a marketing tool that helps companies gauge customer feedback and opinions by using a grading system. The software is an updated alternative to traditional customer satisfaction research to determine customer loyalty. It's a quantitative approach that helps credit unions gauge member satisfaction and commitment. Member Loyalty Group makes it possible for smaller credit unions to achieve their objective of improving services in order to promote increased business and membership.

In Tennessee, two credit unions—ORNL Federal Credit Union and Y12 Federal Credit Union—joined forces to work more efficiently in the insurance space. The CUSO partners are actually competitors in the same market, barely a mile apart in location, but they saw advantages in working together to better serve their members. They formed a company now called 7, which is comprised of two entities, one for general insurance and another for title insurance. By partnering, the credit unions were able to get the scale and volume they needed to be more cost-effective in providing insurance services. It was a vision that required putting aside their local rivalry in the interest of community service. My law firm is proud to have participated in the formation. It's a CUSO success story in which the leadership and staff of both credit unions thrive in the collaboration, to the extent that they won a CUSO of the Year Award.

SCALE = SURVIVAL

Collaboration in CUSOs to create scale is also a matter of survival for individual credit unions. Financial pressures on the credit union business model have led to credit union mergers. The result has been that smaller credit unions are absorbed by larger ones. These mergers of credit unions have been occurring at the rate of almost one a day for the past ten to fifteen years. Credit unions used to number in the tens of thousands, but today there are about 5,500 credit unions nationwide. The primary reason is that credit unions, especially smaller ones, have a difficult time managing the stress of the evolving financial marketplace.

Long-standing credit unions that have served their membership communities for decades have been closing and losing their identities to mergers, all for lack of scale. It's like mom-and-pop shops on Main Street closing their doors and losing community ties due to rising costs and online competitors. The uniqueness of community relationships is being lost in the new marketplace.

Yet this isn't necessary. When a credit union merges with a larger credit union, it is basically finding scale through the merger. The problem is that it has to shut its doors and lose its identity and membership. A far better alternative for achieving scale is for credit unions to collaborate in CUSOs. In this way, credit unions become financial partners. They can share operating expenses, compliance costs, and capital investment to offer new services to their members. Sharing expenses allows credit unions to compete, survive, and maintain their unique connection to their own communities.

Businesses are sometimes hesitant to collaborate with competitors. For credit unions, however, the competition isn't other credit unions but the broader financial marketplace. This includes disruptors in the financial technology space, larger community banks, and regional and national banks. A consumer looking for a mortgage or auto loan can actually avoid banks or their credit union altogether and go online to a fintech company such Lending Club. Online loan services skip the banks, instead sourcing the loan to investors who'll back it up and lend the money.

PayPal is another example of a competitive fintech company in the online financial marketplace. As a payments company, PayPal is fresh competition for traditional banks and credit unions who offer debit cards and credit cards. Shoppers can pay online using PayPal or even make payments to individuals in lieu of plastic or checks. It is innovative financial technology companies like these that have widened consumer options. They are the new competition for both banks and credit unions.

Taking on the competition is TMG Financial Services (TMGFS), a CUSO started by the Iowa Credit Union League. The founder's goal was to give credit unions the ability to retain ownership of their credit card portfolios. TMGFS addresses an underlying problem for credit unions that want to be able to provide credit card loans but don't have adequate resources to take the risk of tying up their liquidity in those loans. Typically, a credit union in this situation will establish an affinity relationship with another financial institution, usually a bank, that becomes the actual lender on the card. The credit union doesn't actually own the portfolio—the bank does—and the credit union gets referral income on the loan. TMGFS was formed with the goal of keeping the portfolio within the credit union community, instead of outsourcing assets to non-credit union banks.

Since coming together as a CUSO, TMGFS is serving one hundred different credit unions and has $150 million in credit card loan assets on their books. Credit unions are providing the liquidity for TMGFS to be able to fund those credit card portfolios. For example, a relatively small credit union with a $10 million credit card portfolio may not have the resources to continue to grow the portfolio themselves. Instead of selling it to a bank, they can sell the portfolio to TMGFS, who will help to manage and grow the portfolio, while allowing the credit union to continue to provide credit card services to their members. At the same time, other credit unions are providing TMGFS with the liquidity to make these services possible for all the associated credit unions. Some of those credit unions are also partners in the CUSO, about ten equity owners in all.

When credit unions form CUSOs, they aren't partnering with the competition. Rather, they are pooling resources in a collaborative financial model. CUSOs allow each credit union partner to maintain their own identity and distinct membership community.

SCALE = EFFICIENCY

Every financial institution has back-office operations, from accounting to IT, loan origination, and servicing to collections and HR support. While there may be some cultural differences from a corporate organizational perspective, the technicalities of providing back-office services and operations are the same. Credit unions are no different, except perhaps for the fact that their entire reason for being isn't the profit motive but to provide the best service to their members.

The question for credit unions, then, is why should they have to single-handedly bear the expenses of providing operational services when there are more cost-effective ways of doing so through collaboration?

One of our clients, Open Technology Solutions (OTS), provides the answer. OTS is a collaboration of three credit unions that partnered to form a CUSO with the objective of pooling their core processing operations. Each originally had their own IT department, their own back-office accounting operations, and their own core processor but decided they'd be better off collaborating and sharing one system together.

They essentially outsourced the operation to their CUSO, calling it Open Technology Solutions. The upshot was, they were able to collectively save up to $1 million per year in costs. Part of that savings came purely from the reduced costs of sharing expenses. However, they were also able to save through their aggregate buying power to negotiate better rates with their outside vendors' software. By partnering in a CUSO, they achieved scale. (For more on OTS, see CUSOs at Work later in this chapter.)

Unfortunately, many credit unions have yet to catch on to the advantages of efficiencies provided by CUSOs. Many are reluctant to give up the autonomy of having their own dedicated operational services. The upshot is that many wind up staring down the barrel of mergers and losing their autonomy altogether. Instead, they should look to collaboration and join with other credit unions in CUSOs that share their same goals of service to members. Credit unions, especially smaller credit unions, need to be working very diligently to find partners with whom they can collaborate to provide more efficient and cost-effective back-office operational services.

HOW TO COLLABORATE

A credit union contemplating partnership in a CUSO needs buy-in across the organization. From leadership to staff, everyone needs to be on board with the strategic goal of collaboration. It requires that management be able to articulate the reasons, purposes, and goals for moving forward with a CUSO. The mission of providing the best service and fiduciary responsibility to members needs to be clearly communicated throughout the credit union.

A credit union's need to take the step to collaborate in a CUSO should be shared and understood as an opportunity for everyone at the credit union.

Fundamental to finding agreement is trust. In my legal practice, we talk about trust all the time. Collaboration is in many ways like a marriage. CUSOs aren't merely business transactions but relationships. Credit unions are entering into a relationship with partners, and those relationships are built on trust.

Building strong, trusting relationships between the management teams of credit union partners is essential to the success of a CUSO. To effectively build that trust, it's important that each credit union has trust in itself. Leadership and staff need to understand and agree on their purpose. They need to establish trust among themselves, trust in their own decision making, and trust in their own mission and shared goals. Only when each credit union in a partnership has strong internal trust can it take that trust forward into relationship with other credit unions.

Too often, we see buy-in from management that doesn't get passed down to different departments and staff within a credit union. For example, credit unions partnering in a mortgage CUSO would need buy-in from each credit union's member service representatives. For the partnership to work, these staff members would need to understand the CUSO's part in their credit union's over-all business model. They would need to be enthusiastic and prepared to refer members to the CUSO for loan origination and processing services.

Buy-in involves commitment along with trust, and that commitment needs to be shared across all individual credit unions. Commitment also needs to extend from each of the credit unions to the CUSO. In order for the partners to reach their goal of scale and reduced costs, they need to be committed to using the services provided by their own CUSO. For a partner to not participate fully in the CUSO's services would be a breach of trust and commitment.

The key to collaboration, therefore, is understanding that there's more to gain than lose. CUSOs offer far more than mere survival to credit unions. Scaling operations and reducing costs by partnering in a CUSO offer distinct benefits, including opportunities for profitability that didn't exist before.

POTENTIAL PROBLEMS

Partnering with other credit unions to attain shared goals requires adaptability. Each partner in a CUSO needs to understand that there are going to be differences of opinion. The ability to adapt to differences and grow in the process will lead to better performance and more successful collaboration. However, it's not always easy for institutions that are used to operating completely on their own to collaborate.

FEAR FACTOR AND CONTROL

Frequently, an organization's management tends to believe they can do things better than anyone else. The senior management team and board members have gotten used to having complete control of their operations. When considering partnership in a CUSO, leadership is essentially considering outsourcing some of that control. Of course, they will have as much control as any other partner in the CUSO, but they will still be giving up complete control of their IT and core processing departments.

There can be fear of losing authority or prestige, and egos can get in the way. It's therefore important to enter into CUSO collaborations with a clear head and definitively articulated goals. CUSOs generally provide their partners with efficient, cost-effective advantages. Yet, there may still be trepidation among the partners. The fear factor can be reduced when all partners are transparent and up front about their goals and expectations for what the CUSO will accomplish.

STAFF CONCERNS

Staff have their own fears and concerns. Staff resistance to collaboration in CUSOs usually centers on their jobs and tenure at their credit union. They become fearful that their positions will soon be redundant and there will be layoffs. Change and reorganization at corporations frequently don't bode well for job security. However, unlike for-profit companies, credit unions walk to the beat of a different drum. It's not the credit union way to lay off staff. A credit union must be transparent and make sure staff understand their roles in this new model. If not, disappointed staff may hinder the success of a collaboration.

In keeping with the credit union tradition of common bonds, credit unions typically want to be good to their employees. They look for creative ways to shift staff into comparable positions at the credit union or at the CUSO. Still, it's understandable that staff may be resistant. There are some real concerns at the staff level; however, CUSOs frequently present new opportunities for advancement. A credit union investing in CUSOs has strategic growth opportunities that may include other opportunities for staff.

UNCLEAR EXPECTATIONS

Some CUSOs are formed with the express purpose of generating profits. In some cases, even back-office operations can turn a profit by selling those services to non-owner credit unions. It's crucial at the outset for the partnering credit unions to have mutually agreed-upon understanding. There's no room for misinterpretation. Every partner needs to be above board about their expectations for the purpose and nature of the collaboration. Is a credit union trying to generate scale and reduce operating expenses? Or is it trying to generate profit and help the credit union's balance sheet through the generation of income?

These are very different and often mutually exclusive goals. The goal of driving down operating expenses is qualitatively different than generating profit. To generate profit requires an operation focused on sales with capital investment in sales staff. Reducing operating expenses, however, involves reduction in staff in order to provide services at a lower cost. Therefore, a credit union whose sole purpose for forming a CUSO is to generate profit shouldn't enter into partnership with a credit union trying to drive down operating expenses.

MANAGEMENT OVERSIGHT

A common error when partnering is neglecting to position dedicated point people from each credit union to oversee the CUSO. Even credit unions with the best intentions make this error. The partners may have worked at establishing trust; they may share a commitment and common purpose, but they haven't adequately dedicated time, resources, and management to running the CUSO. What happens is that managers are pulled in competing directions between their own credit union and the CUSO.

The best approach is for each credit union to dedicate one person, typically an executive team member, to sit on the CUSO's board and provide strategic oversight. This is important because it tethers the CUSO to the partnering credit unions. It helps ensure that the goals of the CUSO remain in line with the goals of the partners. At the same time, the partnering credit unions need to employ an executive manager or CEO with the express purpose of running the CUSO. Just like any organization, a CUSO needs dedicated leadership to ensure that the partners' goals are realized.

It's important to make sure that roles and responsibilities are clearly delineated. The CUSO's executive manager or CEO needs authority to run the company. Credit union representatives on the CUSO board should therefore avoid any attempt or inclination to try to micromanage the CUSO. With these parameters in place, a CUSO is positioned to help credit unions increase their scale by optimizing resources to lower expenses and grow revenue.

COMMON CAUSE

Credit unions have a common purpose, mission, and vision, which is primarily to serve their members and make their financial lives better. With this in mind, it stands to reason that credit unions should be looking for the best ways to cut costs and build efficiencies into their business model through CUSOs. By sticking to the cooperative spirit embedded in the credit union model, credit unions can collaborate with each other to solve shared problems and bring additional benefits to their members. Collaboration is not always easy, but it is the key to a stronger credit union industry.

In the next chapter, we'll look at how CUSOs are collaborating with financial technology innovators for the betterment of credit unions and their members.

CUSOS AT WORK

Open Technology Solutions (OTS) is a successful CUSO, originally formed by four credit unions, now involving three—Bethpage Federal Credit Union, State Employees Credit Union of Maryland, and Bellco Credit Union. Although located in different parts of the country, the three partners share core processing services. Geography wasn't a barrier to their collaboration. Their credit union boards and CEOs got together, shared their goals and aspirations, and developed mutual trust. They agreed that they'd be stronger by sharing specific back-office operations, and OTS was born.

Each partner is a relatively large credit union on its own, and each owns a third of OTS. The CEO of each credit union sits on the board of OTS, and OTS has its own CEO who originally headed IT at Bellco. The partners negotiated a core processing agreement with Fiserv, one of the major providers of core processing systems. Such agreements can be as long as seven years, so the partners had to be sure to coordinate their terms of agreement. With strength in numbers, they were able to negotiate excellent terms for their core processor.

By creating new efficiencies, OTS has been able to save its partners up to $1 million a year in costs. Together, the three credit unions are worth over $15 billion. The CUSO has worked so well that the partners have decided to collaborate on another CUSO to perform mortgage servicing and originations, collections, and call center operations. These various back-office operations will be outsourced collaboratively to their new CUSO called S3.

Things worked out so well for OTS that other clients at our law firm decided to follow their example. Three credit unions in New Jersey—Aspire Federal Credit Union, United Teletech Financial Federal Credit Union, and Credit Union of New Jersey—partnered to form Member Support Services (MSS). They are smaller credit unions than the OTS partners, but together they're worth just under $1 billion.

The partners originally met at a national credit union conference in Washington, DC, and brainstormed a concept for their CUSO on a bar napkin. Not only were they inspired by the example of OTS, but they also worked with the CEO of OTS in the early stages to help formulate plans for their own CUSO. The credit union space is a very collegial environment, and CUSOs are more than happy to share experiences and advice.

MSS is built on the model of both OTS and S3. It was formed as a CUSO that combines the functions of core processing and back-office operations within one company. In addition to IT, mortgages, and a call center, MSS handles communications and telephone systems, and they are looking at insurance services as well. The CEOs of each credit union sit on the MSS board, and they hired a dedicated CEO to run their CUSO. MSS is an example of smaller institutions coming together to collaborate, save money, and do more than just survive—they want to thrive in the new financial marketplace.

CHAPTER FOUR

CUSOS AND TECHNOLOGICAL INNOVATION

We explored how credit unions collaborate with one another to gain scale and drive down costs to provide better service for their members. They do this through CUSOs to bring new efficiencies to their back-office operations, such as IT and loan origination. Now we'll look at how credit unions partner with entrepreneurs in the field of financial technology, or "fintech," to provide more innovative and efficient customer-facing services.

THE FINTECH REVOLUTION

Since the dawn of the internet and the advent of online banking and mobile devices, disruptors have revolutionized the banking industry. In the new digital era, the traditional banking model has become obsolete and given way to innovation by technology entrepreneurs who develop innovative applications that bring the convenience of financial services directly to customers.

These changes follow similar changes in other industries. Twenty years ago, the standard for home video entertainment was DVD rental stores epitomized by the ubiquitous Blockbuster chain. As streaming video technology became available, video rental was supplanted by on-demand streaming services such as Netflix and Hulu, offering the sheer convenience of instant digital viewing; and as the internet grew in speed and availability, Blockbuster was soon out of business. The popular bookstore chain Borders suffered a similar fate at the hands of online bookselling by the retail giant Amazon. Both Blockbuster and Borders fell by the wayside because they failed to anticipate, innovate, and plan for relevancy as the rules of the game began to change.

Similar disruption has occurred in the taxi industry, which used to be tightly regulated by municipalities that doled out limited and expensive taxicab licenses. Along came Uber and Lyft with innovative software applications and ride sharing that allowed individuals to hire and pay for rides by smartphone. Gone are the days of exclusive yellow cab monopolies and hailing cabs on street corners in the rain.

In the financial services industry, technological innovation has led to advancements both in back-office operations and at the front end of customer service. These customer-facing innovations are bringing together new CUSO partnerships among credit unions and fintech entrepreneurs. The cliché of the young Silicon Valley tech developer with a new product or service to sell has some basis in fact, although tech entrepreneurs can be of any age and hail from anywhere. What's critical to technology developers, however, is that they don't always have the funds to further develop and bring their product to market on their own. They also don't always have a captive group of people to use the product and help improve it. This is where credit unions are playing a vital role. Just as credit unions learned to work together to solve problems and drive down costs in the back office, fintech innovators and credit unions have come together to make financial services more efficient and convenient.

Technology developers are looking to fill needs in industries that require better processes and functionality in their products and services. PayPal and Lending Club are examples of financial technologies applied to online payments and loan services. Both are fintech operations that have raised the bar of competition for traditional banks and credit unions. Venmo, the "digital wallet," facilitates person-to-person transactions. Square is a company that simplifies credit card transactions via handheld devices. Fintech startups like these are changing the game. Major competitors such as Apple, Google, and Samsung, that aren't even traditional players in financial services, are all innovating with their own mobile pay products. As consumer options expand in the fintech arena, so are partnerships among tech developers and credit unions in the form of CUSOs.

An example of these CUSO partnerships is the bank transfer and payment company called Dwolla. When the founders of Dwolla were just getting started in Iowa, they ran into a few roadblocks. As a startup, they needed seed money to finance their product development. They also needed to partner with a financial institution in order to facilitate the transfer money, otherwise they'd have to obtain licenses to move money in each state individually. Financial institutions, such as banks and credit unions, are already chartered to move funds across all fifty states.

The entrepreneurs at Dwolla reached out to people they knew in the credit union industry and wound up teaming with the Veridian Credit Union, as well as an existing CUSO called The Members Group, owned by the Iowa Credit Union League. In this way, they obtained the funding they needed for development along with access to electronic transfer origination and processing. Dwolla is a prime example of how a fintech startup teamed with the credit union industry to become a CUSO with the investment and back-office support of its credit union partners.

JOINING THE COMPETITION

Credit unions haven't traditionally been in the business of moving money. They have always been more about member services, primarily savings and loans. Income varies considerably among different credit unions, but the big moneymaker for credit unions over recent decades has been income generated by "interchange." This is essentially income earned on transactions by members using their credit union credit cards and debit cards. Just like banks, credit unions make a few cents on transactions made by credit or debit at stores or online. But with new competition from payment services such as PayPal and Apple Pay, credit unions are losing income from card fees. This pressure is intensified by the future possibility of transactions without use of credit or debit cards. It has therefore become important for credit unions to capitalize on the latest innovative financial services technologies.

In the online marketplace, for example, innovative companies such as SoFi and Lending Club are streamlining the lending process. Consumers can go online and get a loan in minutes. The traditional model used by banks and credit unions has always involved underwriting and processing that can take a week to generate a loan. Even then, an applicant can be turned down for approval because their risk level is considered too high. Tech innovators looked at that problem and created underwriting algorithms that allow lenders to generate loans in as little as thirty seconds. Their software draws on information from public records and pulls an applicant's credit history in record time. It's a whole lot quicker than filling out a loan application at a bank or credit union, answering a bunch of questions, and waiting a week for a decision. Credit unions don't want to be left behind and watch their loan business go to online lenders.

Cryptocurrencies such as Bitcoin and Ripple are causing further disruption to the traditional banking model. They have the potential to undercut the entire currency system, creating new problems for credit unions. It's therefore essential for credit unions to be on their toes and partnering with financial innovators.

At the same time, credit unions are starting to embrace Big Data and predictive analytics to help anticipate the needs of their members. The alternative is to wind up as a Blockbuster or Borders when Amazon comes on the scene. Amazon is a powerhouse of gathering and analyzing data to profile customer buying habits and determine their wants and needs. It's the digital extension of traditional in-store endcaps and displays, but far superior, because data analytics curates products for individual customers.

Fintech innovators are using data and predictive analytics to develop financial services streamlined for consumers. Through CUSO partnerships with fintech entrepreneurs, credit unions are now getting past the old school paradigm of tellers behind windows and mortgage lenders sitting behind desks waiting for potential borrowers to enter their branch office. In the digital environment, borrowers will look online for loans first because it's easier.

Historically, credit unions were actually disruptors of their own when they came into existence almost a hundred years ago. They recognized an existing problem in communities that needed loans that banks wouldn't give them. Banks didn't consider farmers and factory workers good credit risks. So, people banded together in credit unions to pool their resources and lend to each other. It is this tradition of innovation that credit unions are exercising once more in the new financial marketplace through CUSOs.

My legal practice assisted in the formation of one such online loan service, QCash Financial, a CUSO formed by the Washington State Employees Credit Union (WSECU). QCash was founded as an affordable alternative to the exorbitant costs of loans generated by payday lenders. Payday loans are very short term, typically designed to be paid off within two weeks but at very high interest rates. They are secured by the borrower's paycheck, so they are almost like a pay advance with extra costs built in. At interest rates comparable to 1,000 percent, it's no wonder that payday loans are considered predatory.

When WSECU analyzed the lending market in their area, they found that even their own members were getting payday loans, even though the credit union had the capacity to provide far better, affordable short-term loans. They decided to develop software using algorithms to automate the loan process. The online program made it possible to underwrite a loan quickly on the day a member needs money. QCash Financial has worked to serve its borrowers fairly and efficiently. It illustrates how a credit union can see a problem and use leading-edge technology to find a solution to meet its members' pressing needs.

Another consideration for credit unions is that the fastest growing segment of consumers are the younger generations. These are the wired generations that credit unions need to reach in order to expand their membership. These generations are characterized by a community-oriented focus, activism, volunteerism, and buying local. They are natural customers for credit unions.

During the financial crisis of 2008–2009, these young people embodied the anti-Wall Street protests. They were anti-bank and called themselves 99 percenters in opposition to the status quo and wide income disparities. Credit unions took notice and organized a National Bank Transfer Day, saying, "Hey, we're a different kind of financial institution; we're cooperatives; we're the alternative. You can take action by transferring your bank account to a local credit union." The ranks of credit union members expanded to more than 100 million during that time.

The key point is that financial innovation is not waiting. Credit unions need to accelerate CUSO partnerships with fintech entrepreneurs who are poised to generate the next wave of innovation. By bringing value to their members, credit unions can drive growth. Mobile technology coupled with the cooperative spirit can be a huge win-win for credit unions in the digital age.

STRATEGIES FOR INNOVATION

To stay relevant and survive, credit unions are embracing CUSOs as vehicles for innovation. With fintech partners, they are innovating and creating products and services that are more functional, faster, and easier to use. The potential for credit unions in this arena is manifold. They can be both owners of the product and users of the product. Through CUSOs, they also gain strategic input into the innovation to help ensure that it will meet the needs of their members.

Fintech partnering through CUSOs is vital because on a legal basis, credit unions can only partner through CUSOs. By statute, they can't form businesses any other way. If a credit union wants to invest in innovation and financial technology, it can only do so by investing in CUSOs or in a company that's willing to become a CUSO. The credit union becomes an owner or equity holder of that company, and the company immediately becomes a CUSO and has to comply with CUSO regulations.

CUSOs are required to primarily serve credit unions and credit union members. This can be potentially restrictive. However, CUSO partnerships are attractive to fintech entrepreneurs because it's easier than trying to partner with national banks. Credit unions also have a built-in customer base. For their part, credit unions are highly motivated to have strategic input and a stake in the game. Fintech partnerships give credit unions access to a knowledge base and tech expertise through investment. CUSO partnerships give them more control over delivery channels and access points, such as mobile applications for their members. As owners or investors, credit unions have input in the early stages of technology development. It's much different than buying an existing application from a vendor where there's little control over access points for their members.

Fintech entrepreneurs often need access to money for development and credit unions give them that access, along with a captive customer base. The service is pushed out to credit union members. From the entrepreneur's perspective, there's immediate strategic access to users, which is crucial to success, because it drives up the value of the company. An added incentive is that the entrepreneur becomes an inside player in the credit union industry through the CUSO. It brings some degree of prestige by association, or branding in the marketing sense. The entrepreneur gains an inside track and access to other credit unions that may be interested in partnership or becoming clients.

For example, CU Rate Reset is a CUSO partnership that helps credit union members modify loans. It's based on software developed by fintech entrepreneurs who wanted to help financial institutions retain loan assets, such as mortgages and auto loans. Rate Reset offers a remedy to the problem incurred by the risk of loans going into default. The software lets a loan recipient lower the amount of their monthly loan payment to a more affordable amount. The borrower does this online using a rate meter on the company's website.

In the world of auto loans, for instance, car buyers frequently receive financing at the dealer. The dealer usually sells the loan to a lending institution, which could be a bank or a credit union. If the borrower later finds it difficult to make their monthly loan payments, the loan could go into default. This is where Rate Reset enters the picture. The company's software contacts borrowers by email or text offering them the opportunity to adjust their loan payments to fit their budget.

When Rate Reset's developers became interested in partnering with credit unions, they reached out to my law firm to help develop a structure for credit unions to invest in their company. The CUSO they formed is comprised of credit union investors, along with the founders, who maintain a majority position in the company. Rate Reset follows the CUSO business model of serving the credit union industry. The company serves members of the partnering credit unions and also has contractual relationships with other credit unions to serve their members. Rate Reset actively reaches out to credit union members offering the opportunity to refinance their loans or mortgages at better rates.

Credit unions and financial services innovators are teaming up to find new strategies for solving problems through products and services that address member needs. By forming fintech CUSOs, credit unions capitalize on both investment and strategic input.

COLLABORATING WITH INNOVATORS

The nature of partnering with entrepreneurs to form CUSOs is different than credit unions partnering with each other. When credit unions collaborate to save expenses on back-office operations, they come together in CUSOs as cooperatives without a profit or investment motive. When credit unions form CUSOs with fintech developers, however, they are investing in companies whose goals are making money and finding clients. They solve problems and meet clients' needs with innovative products and services, and at the same time they drive up the value of the CUSO and generate income. In partnering with developers, credit unions receive income and equity, but profitability isn't their primary focus. They are more interested in driving quality service for their members.

As credit unions and entrepreneurs come together in CUSOs, it's therefore important for them to understand and think through potential differences. They need to be clear on their goals and objectives and on how they can align in the same direction. For one thing, there are certain regulatory hurdles that all partners should be aware of when forming CUSOs. Entrepreneurs should be clear from the start about the obligations involved in forming CUSOs and the implications as the company grows.

It's also important to know that every CUSO has its own unique circumstances and players. Some entrepreneurs are driven primarily by a desire for people to use their service. Profit may be a secondary consideration; they may not expect immediate or short-term financial profit. In fact, they may be thinking that the company isn't likely to yield profit during the first four to five years. Their greater concern may be finding users, providing new financial tools, and improving the quality of their product. They may be more concerned with finding the funding to continue to craft their product and make it great. In some situations, credit unions are motivated to generate value and profit through investment.

It's always hard to generalize. Through my own experience, I've found that the motivations of CUSO partners in the technology field can vary. What is vital, however, is that all parties to a partnership practice due diligence in understanding and assessing where they stand when it comes to their intentions and goals for the investment. Are they more motivated by service to members, by making money, or by the technology itself? The partners may fall at different places on a continuum of priorities.

Typically, a fintech developer is working on a solution to a problem and needs financing. If we apply this scenario to the popular TV investment show *Shark Tank*, it might look something like this: a financial innovator pitches his idea to potential investors, who in this case are credit unions. Typically, the entrepreneur needs capital to continue development of his product. The potential investors ask questions and try to assess the company's true value and potential. The entrepreneur tells the credit unions what he thinks the company is presently worth and what percentage of investment he's looking to sell.

For credit unions that invest in CUSOs, these partnerships can help their balance sheets in two ways. First, there's income potential from being an equity owner in the company, whether that income comes through net profits or appreciation of the investment. Second, when a credit union provides innovative services to its members, there's potential for growth both in membership and in the services those members use, such as loans. Value isn't always in the form of an increase in equity over time. A successful CUSO can generate value through both equity appreciation and a great balance sheet. Credit unions and their fintech partners benefit from both net income and the CUSO's appreciation in value.

A CUSO's product can serve members of both the invested credit unions and other credit unions whose members use the product. Income is generated through these relationships. This drives income to the CUSO's balance sheet. It could also generate an actual dividend and distribution of profit to the credit union as an owner and shareholder in the CUSO. The credit union's members would then receive dividends in the form of interest on their savings accounts. At the end of the year, some credit unions, though not all, will issue special dividends to their members according to the size of their deposits.

In time, of course, a credit union can decide to separate from the CUSO and sell its appreciated equity interest in the company. Another eventuality is that all the CUSO partners decide to sell the company together and each receives their share of the increased value of investment.

CREDIT UNIONS INNOVATING FOR THEMSELVES

As new financial technologies come to market, it's crucial for credit unions to be mindful and aware of trends. Credit unions don't want to be caught standing on the sidelines watching business potential slip by. In fact, credit unions can sometimes carry the ball themselves by developing innovative ways to improve service for their own members. They may have the expertise on staff to develop a new software application, or they can hire independent contract developers to improve their operations. For example, an IT staff member at one credit union developed a creative adaptation of their in-branch video advertising systems. My law firm helped the credit union form a CUSO to market the innovation to other credit unions.

Another example involves several credit unions partnering in a fintech CUSO without a third-party entrepreneur. Constellation Digital Partners started with an idea floated by the management team of Coastal Federal Credit Union in North Carolina. It started with several what-ifs. What if we had the ability to provide for ourselves all the functions of online and mobile banking? What if we set up our own consistent digital platform for our members to interact with the credit union? What if that platform allowed members to still, like today, see their accounts and transactions, pay bills, transfer money, and make loan payments but could possibly do so much more? What if we built a platform that allowed us to create front-end services digitally for other credit unions? What if we allow anyone to develop services that could be used by members through our front end?

Those questions spawned Constellation. It started with a due diligence expense-sharing agreement among a dozen or so credit unions and credit union service providers to fund a proof of concept in order to see whether the idea would work. The platform that resulted is a digital serving platter of services that credit unions can provide to their members. It's a system that allows for the continued development of products and services that can be delivered to credit union members directly through the platform. The partners formed Constellation as a CUSO and raised about $30 million to keep moving the process forward. Coastal Federal's CIO became Constellation's CEO, and the first live use of the platform is slated for 2018. Constellation points to the possibilities open to credit unions in the fintech marketplace through CUSOs.

Smart credit unions are keeping a close eye on innovation, especially in the sphere of mobile banking applications. Credit unions need to be attending fintech and CUSO conferences where they can network with innovators and other credit unions about solutions to shared problems. The history and experience of credit unions show that shared problems lead to shared solutions.

CUSOS AT WORK

OnApproach is a CUSO based in the Minneapolis/St. Paul area of Minnesota. It began as the innovative concept of a fintech entrepreneur who saw opportunity in the credit union space.

The entrepreneur had a background in data modeling and architecture in other industries. His concept was to help financial institutions build their own data warehouses to collect, store, and analyze their data. One of his first customers was a credit union for which he developed data architecture tailored specifically to that credit union. While doing this, he realized there were a lot of other credit unions that weren't capitalizing on the vast amount of data they collected. So he formed a company, called it OnApproach, and started looking for more opportunities among credit unions.

The founder approached my law firm to assist him in partnering with credit unions. He'd built a very complex and detailed warehouse structure for data integration and analytics that would meet the needs of credit unions, and he decided to go beyond just being a service provider. We helped him structure his company and connected him with several credit unions that might be interested in investing in a company like OnApproach. The CUSO is now fully invested and serving credit unions across the country. But there's more to the story.

Another client of ours is Deep Future Analytics, a CUSO that was formed by the Denali Federal Credit Union in Alaska. Deep Future was also working on ways to analyze credit union data and floated the idea of partnering with OnApproach. The partnership made perfect sense, as the two companies could collaborate on collecting and analyzing data.

An added component of the partnership is the contribution of another entrepreneur with expertise in predictive modeling analytics. Applied to financial services, predictive analytics makes it possible to predict consumer behavior in services such as auto loans. It can determine the likelihood of default, attrition, refinancing, or paying off the loan.

Predictive analytics allows credit unions to move beyond traditional lending models, such as credit scores that show only past performance. In partnership, the two companies can aggregate all the data from OnApproach's clients into one pool that feeds the predictive models. The more data available, the more accurate the models.

This CUSO partnership was a natural relationship and an innovative and creative venture to better serve union members in the expanding digital marketplace.

CHAPTER FIVE

FORMING A CUSO

Successful CUSOs, like other companies, begin with a shared vision. It's therefore crucial that credit unions and other founding partners share and align their vision to meet mutual goals and needs. By their very definition, CUSOs also need to meet the needs of credit union members.

There are basically four ways a credit union can align itself in a CUSO:

1. JOIN AN EXISTING CUSO

The first way is to invest in a CUSO that has already been formed. The CUSO has been established by one or more credit unions and is providing services to meet their collective needs. The existing CUSO presents an opportunity for other credit unions that also wish to join and gain strategic advantage.

2. FORM ITS OWN CUSO

A second option is for a credit union to form its own CUSO to provide services to its own members and often to members of other credit unions as well. In this case, the CUSO is like an operating subsidiary of the credit union.

3. FORM A CUSO WITH OTHER CREDIT UNIONS

Several credit unions can decide to collaborate in the formation of a CUSO to meet their collective needs. They come together to drive down costs for operating expenses, such as core processing systems and IT. They accomplish this by forming a CUSO to share the expenses, pooling resources for stronger, more robust, and effective systems and staff.

4. INVEST IN TECHNOLOGY OR SERVICE

Credit unions can also invest in an existing company providing a service or product that serves the credit union industry. Entrepreneurs in the financial services industry are often looking for investments to further develop their products and services. If an investment comes from a credit union, then the company becomes a CUSO.

BUSINESS PLANNING AND STRUCTURE

When I meet with CUSO founding partners, I always

emphasize that a CUSO begins with a well-conceived business plan. A CUSO's concept, vision, and mission should be fleshed out, along with goals for what the partners wish to accomplish strategically and operationally. Some basic questions I ask involve the founders' goals: Are they looking for scale and efficiencies? Are they looking for profits? Are they looking to offer new services to credit union members?

Planning starts with a meeting of minds. When a CUSO's vision and goals are clearly established at the outset, the CUSO can be structured to meet them. If the company's primary goal is efficiencies, the CUSO's management team can work to meet those expectations. If the goal is new member services, management will want to maximize return on new investment.

Structuring CUSOs isn't very complex. A CUSO's structure is dependent on its ownership, whether one or more credit unions are involved or whether it's a joint venture that includes fintech entrepreneurs or other non-credit union partners. When all parties are aligned at the outset, when they know their roles and what's expected of them, the company can be structured on firm footing.

LIMITED LIABILITY COMPANIES

CUSOs are usually formed as limited liability companies

(LLCs). In most states, it's a very simple process, requiring only a one- or two-page document filed for a low fee. From a tax perspective, an LLC can be treated as a pass-through entity; its owners are taxed individually based on their share of the profits. Credit unions, however, by virtue of their nonprofit status, are not taxed. This contrasts with a C corporation in which the corporation itself pays taxes on the profits.

OPERATING AGREEMENTS

By their nature, LLCs are flexible in structure. I always recommend that an LLC start with an operating agreement, very much like the bylaws of a corporation. (In some states, these are called member control agreements or regulations.) The operating agreement allows for flexibility in structuring the CUSO. In contrast with rigid rules at the state level for C corporations, provisions of operating agreements for LLCs are minimal.

In the CUSO environment, where there is usually more than one owner, an LLC's operating agreement should include all the details of the company's structure. It should describe board composition and whether board members are elected or appointed. For example, an operating agreement would specify whether a majority owner can appoint three board members, while other partners appoint two. It would also define profits and losses and how they are to be shared among the owners. The operating agreement is where the details of an exit strategy are laid out, including the ability to remove an owner for not supporting the CUSO's services.

CUSO MANAGEMENT

CUSOs are usually managed by a board of directors. In small CUSOs, each partner usually makes a fixed number of board appointments. In larger CUSOs, board members are usually elected.

When establishing a new CUSO, it's vital to plan for the most effective management structure. Credit union partners, whose primary interests are member service and efficiency, as well as reputation, are inclined to place more importance on management. For practical purposes, a board of no more than seven to nine members is effective. Keeping a board small allows for quicker decision making.

The day-to-day management of a CUSO is generally delegated to a CEO or manager. In instances where there is a majority equity owner, often they have the most influence on who is the CEO or manager. When a CUSO is founded by a fintech developer with credit union partners, it's often the entrepreneur who becomes the CEO.

COMPETING EXPECTATIONS

Credit unions are from Venus and entrepreneurs are from Mars. In other words, they come from different places ideologically and approach CUSO partnerships with different expectations. Credit unions enter from the nonprofit sector where service is more important than profits. Entrepreneurs look to capitalize on their investments, whether through distributions, dividends, or the eventual sale of the company.

As nonprofit cooperatives, any money that credit unions make goes back into serving their members. This doesn't mean that credit unions don't want to make money, but rather that no individual gets rich off the profits. When entrepreneurs invest, however, eventual profits are what they're looking for. They may want to build their idea for five or ten years, then sell and move on.

As we've seen, credit unions look at CUSOs more as long-term investments with no horizon. They don't invest with the intent of selling or divesting. Their goals are more service oriented. They want to see their investment appreciate so they can show an increase in assets on their balance sheets, but what they really want to see is a positive effect on member service.

It's an interesting dichotomy for credit unions that partner with for-profit investors. The CUSO partnership will require a clear vision from the outset. During the planning stages, the partners will come to terms with competing expectations of driving profits and providing cheaper rates for member services. There may be differences even among credit union partners who place different weight on profit and service.

Another difference between credit unions and entrepreneurs involves tax law. By virtue of their nonprofit status, credit unions are not taxed on their CUSO income. However, entrepreneur partners are taxed. Consider a CUSO formed as an LLC that is comprised of one credit union partner and one fintech developer, each with 50 percent ownership. The CUSO earns $100,000 in net profit during a single year, so each partner receives $50,000 in profit. The credit union is tax exempt, so all they have to do is recognize the profit on their books; they don't have to pay taxes. The entrepreneur, however, will have to recognize $50,000 in income on his personal income taxes. The CUSO may not want to distribute all the profits. Instead, it may wish to keep its cash on hand to continue to fund operations. The CUSO can handle the entrepreneur's tax liability by distributing cash to only cover the tax burden. The entrepreneur's share of capital will be slightly discounted to account for this tax distribution.

During the lifetime of a CUSO, the focus can shift and partner perspectives can change. A credit union may become more interested in profit than when they started. There may be changes in management with evolving points of view. Newer managers may look at the CUSO and wonder why it isn't turning a profit. Credit union partners may want additional services at cheaper rates, while entrepreneurs just want greater monetary return. These differences can be exacerbated when new investors are brought into established CUSOs. Therefore, a CUSO's vision, mission, and goals need to be clearly articulated and understood by all parties. A discussion about expectations should be part of the original vision for the company. The vision should address profits, management structure, and whether new investors will be added in the future.

For a CUSO to be successful, differing points of view need to be reconciled at the outset. Every investor, credit union, and entrepreneur needs to be up front about their goals and expectations to be sure they are aligned. However, goals can change over time, and this is where having a good exit strategy comes into play.

STOCK OPTIONS AND INCENTIVES

Profit sharing with employees is a relatively new concept for CUSOs. It's typically more suited to CUSOs that have an exit horizon, usually an eventual sale or public offering. This isn't usually the case with CUSOs comprised exclusively of credit union partners that operate in the nonprofit arena. However, as a growing number of CUSOs form in partnership with fintech developers, profit sharing is becoming more common.

Technology CUSOs, in particular, may be motivated to provide key employees with incentives to stay with the company and strive toward revenue and growth goals. Some CUSOs are now offering profit sharing based on success milestones, putting some profits aside for staff, and the rest back into the company.

Again, focus on the vision of the CUSO and make sure that employee incentives fit within that vision. Make sure that the metrics and economics of those incentives run parallel to the goals and objectives of the CUSO. We want to make sure that employees and the owners of the CUSO are all rowing the boat in the same direction. To this end, employee incentives are a good tool if created appropriately.

EXIT STRATEGY

Planning exit strategies before a CUSO is even operational might seem to sow doubt about a CUSO's success, but it's sort of like prenuptial planning. The future may look blissful, but before the venture is finalized, it's important to plan ahead for possible unwinding. Partners can be optimistic and plan to work hard to achieve success, but fallback considerations can't be ignored. When push comes to shove, differences of opinion can arise. CUSOs, therefore, need to be structured so that a partner can leave amicably. In addition, sometimes CUSOs run their natural course and are no longer serving their initial useful purpose. There should also be provisions for an eventual winding down of the CUSO in its entirety.

A partner that is no longer using a CUSO's services can be a drag on the company and undermine its growth. A good way to avoid this situation is to build safeguards and triggers into the operating agreement. The process should be fair and transparent. Often, the best way to handle this dynamic is to plan for a supermajority of the owners, or a large portion of the board, to make the determination. The board can then remove the credit union as an owner, sometimes even involuntarily.

A stipulation can be built into the agreement that the departing partner receives something in return for their equity interest in the CUSO. This exchange for equity could take the form of a return of the book value of the investment or an agreement to determine the fair market value of the interest in the CUSO.

Issues of valuation can be very expensive and speculative. This is why it's important to consider exit strategies at the outset when the company is formed. Situations can arise where a second valuation is demanded. This is all best avoided when addressed in advance during the CUSO planning stage. The business plan can establish at the outset a method for calculating fair market value.

Planning an exit strategy in advance induces partners to think hard about their goals and expectations for the CUSO, and can ensure a stronger, more forward-looking company.

COMMON PROBLEMS

The goals and needs of partners who form CUSOs can change over time. The efficiencies a CUSO once provided to a credit union partner can change. At some point, there may be a scale flip and it may be more advantageous for a credit union to bring the CUSO's service in-house for more control and flexibility. A credit union can grow to the point that the CUSO stops being cost-effective.

Another concern would be the situation of a partner who is speculatively investing in the CUSO without planning to participate beyond their initial financial investment. This could be problematic for other credit union partners who may be making larger investments and fully intend to use the CUSO's services. Situations like this should be avoided at the outset in order to prevent conflict later on.

Usually, only one or two organizations or individuals

are deeply involved in driving the project forward. They attempt to make it work by all means necessary. If other partners aren't focusing on the CUSO, or aren't using the CUSO's services, they may sit on the sidelines for quite some time. Such partners are a drag on the CUSO's efficiencies right from the start. To be successful, CUSO partnerships require all hands on deck to help implement its operations and services. This needs to be understood by all parties who enter into the CUSO agreement.

Usually, credit unions that enter CUSO partnerships are highly motivated. It should be understood, however, that CUSO partnerships are often driven by the passion of individuals. Due to their enthusiasm, these cheerleaders may not be inclined to consider potential problems. They may be wary that bringing up sticking points could derail the entire enterprise before it starts. In the funding and formation stage, these key people want to focus on getting the CUSO done. They don't want potential partners to say, "Well, you've convinced me not to do it." It's far better and wiser to lay all cards on the table and find partners of like mind and mutual vision.

PASSION + PLANNING = SUCCESS

Using CUSOs as part of a credit union business model is essential, but it isn't easy. A credit union needs to plan and strategize for the success of the CUSO. The key is passion for the project, leadership, and understanding the purpose of the CUSO before the credit union dives in. With these requisite factors in place, success should not be hard to come by.

CHAPTER SIX

THE REGULATORY REALM OF CUSOS

When a credit union invests in a company, that company, by definition, becomes a CUSO. All parties entering into a CUSO need to understand that although CUSOs are not directly regulated by the credit union regulators, there are still regulations to be followed. It's therefore important to be aware of the current regulatory climate. It's also important to have a solid understanding of whom a CUSO can serve as customers and what services a CUSO is permitted to provide.

WHO REGULATES CUSOS?

As we saw in Chapter One, credit unions are chartered at the state or federal levels. CUSOs, however, aren't governed by the same tight regulations as individual credit unions, and this is how they provide access to more flexible product and service markets. Yet even with greater latitude and more elbow room to enter into business partnerships, credit unions are responsible to ensure that their CUSOs are in compliance with regulations.

DIRECT VS. INDIRECT REGULATORS

Federally chartered credit unions are regulated directly by the National Credit Union Administration (NCUA), while state-chartered credit unions are directly regulated by the state in which they are chartered. CUSOs, however, aren't *directly* regulated by either federal or state credit union authorities. They are only regulated *indirectly* because of their association with credit unions. It's the credit union's responsibility to make sure that its CUSOs follow the applicable regulatory requirements and obligations. Generally, this is done through an agreement between the credit union investor and the CUSO, whereby the CUSO agrees to comply with certain regulations.

The NCUA can hold federally chartered credit unions to task for the operations of any CUSO they form or join. For state-chartered credit unions, it's the individual state's banking authority that holds credit unions to task for their CUSOs. The one area of exception to state versus federal charters concerns deposit insurance. All credit unions are monitored for safety and soundness through the NCUA. As mentioned in Chapter One, credit unions are insured by the National Credit Union Share Insurance Fund. Every federally chartered credit union is required to have share insurance, and most state-chartered credit unions are required by their states to also carry federal share insurance (some states allow private insurance). So when it comes to deposit insurance and the soundness of the federal insurance fund, the NCUA does have some indirect authority over CUSOs at both the federal and state levels.

All state-chartered credit unions also have their own state authority that examines them. When it comes to CUSOs, many state regulatory agencies simply follow NCUA regulations. This practice may be formally stated through statute or regulation, or it may be done informally with state regulators using the NCUA regulations as the basis for their decisions. Some states have passed their own CUSO regulations, and in most cases, those regulations are very similar to the NCUA's, with some variation.

All credit unions are limited by regulation as to the amount of money they can invest in CUSOs. Federally chartered credit unions can invest up to 1 percent of their total assets in CUSOs. That investment is in the aggregate, so it includes the sum total of a credit union's investment in all CUSOs. A credit union with $100 million in assets could invest up to $1 million of those assets in CUSOs. For state-chartered credit unions, some states set the limit at the same 1 percent, although some states go as high as 10 percent of assets in the aggregate.

The upshot is that when a credit union enters into a CUSO, it takes on a certain amount of risk. That risk could ultimately affect the credit union itself, so both state and federal regulators will hold the credit union accountable and institute investment limitations.

BUSINESS REGULATIONS

CUSOs are companies doing business, and as businesses, they must follow regulations governing the particular industry in which they operate. In this sense, CUSOs are regulated just like other businesses in their industry, regardless of being a CUSO.

For example, a CUSO that is providing insurance services would need to be licensed to sell insurance just like any other insurance agency, whether owned by a credit union or not. It would be regulated by the insurance authorities of the particular states in which it does business. A CUSO that is providing mortgage loans to borrowers in all fifty states would need to be licensed in each of those states. A CUSO that is a broker-dealer for retail securities would be subject to state and federal regulators, such as the Securities and Exchange Commission (SEC), and independent authorities such as the Financial Industry Regulatory Authority (FINRA).

THREE PILLARS OF REGULATION

There are three distinct areas, what I call "pillars," of the federal CUSO investment regulations that apply to credit unions and their investment in CUSOs. In the event that a federally chartered credit union investor fails to ensure that a CUSO complies with these regulations, the NCUA could insist that the credit union divest. Therefore, when a credit union invests in or lends to a CUSO, it is important to stipulate that the CUSO will follow these regulations.

The three pillars of regulation include:

- Permissible Services
- Customer Base (Who are the CUSO's primary customers?)
- Legal Administrative Requirements

All three pillars apply to federally chartered credit unions, but only the third pillar applies to state-chartered credit unions as well. When it comes to the first two pillars, some states will defer to NCUA regulations, but others will use their own laws.

PERMISSIBLE SERVICES

According to NCUA regulations, a credit union can invest in a company (thus making it a CUSO) if the CUSO agrees to only provide "permissible services." Permissible services involve certain distinct categories, but there is still wiggle room. For instance, one category is "loan support services." These services can be quite diverse, such as brokering loans, collecting on defaulted loans, or holding real estate owned (REO) properties that didn't sell at foreclosure auction. All these activities, among others, fall under the broad category of loan support services.

The services that CUSOs are permitted to provide are generally related to and supportive of credit union services and operations. This is why the name CUSO stands for "credit union service organization." CUSOs are meant to support credit unions and their members. These services generally relate to the types of financial services that credit unions provide. The NCUA regulation concerning permissible services is set up as a list of approximately twenty general categories. It's not meant to be specific.

For example, CUSOs can perform services that fall into broad service categories, such as management services, real estate services, insurance services, financial counseling services, electronic transaction services, payroll processing services, and securities brokerage services. The categories of services are meant to be descriptive, allowing for many different services to possibly fit under one or more of the categories. It is also important to note that a CUSO can provide more than one permissible service. Credit unions therefore have some room to innovate within the general categories of permissible services. As we've seen, CUSOs have been formed to do electronic transaction services, credit card and payment processing, data processing, and Automated Clearing House (ACH)-type transfers.

Insurance is a particularly interesting area in that credit unions themselves aren't permitted to operate as insurance brokerages. However, CUSOs can operate as insurance brokers. So if a credit union wants to get into the insurance industry, the only way it can do so is through a CUSO. The same dynamic holds for real estate. CUSOs can be real estate brokers, but credit unions cannot.

In a general sense, permissible services for CUSOs relate to the financial industry; after all, credit unions are financial institutions. CUSOs will generally either expand or support the products and services that a credit union already provides, allowing a credit union to better serve all its members' financial needs.

If a service doesn't conform to one of the permissible NCUA categories, then it's a service a CUSO can't provide. As an example, CUSOs can originate several different types of loans but not all loans. Under the regulations, permissible loan originations are commercial loans or business loans, residential mortgage loans, student loans, and credit card loans. Specifically missing from the permissible list for CUSOs are some loans that credit unions can originate but CUSOs cannot, such as auto loans and unsecured loans.

Remember the example of the CUSO called Rate Reset described in Chapter Four? Rate Reset offers credit union members the opportunity to modify their loans, particularly auto loans, but credit unions actually make the loans. This is in keeping with NCUA regulations that don't allow CUSOs to originate auto loans. The services provided by Rate Reset would fall under several different categories, such as loan support services, electronic transaction services, and/or marketing and management services.

Another CUSO described in Chapter Four, QCash Financial, is an affordable alternative to the exorbitant costs of unsecured loans generated by payday lenders. It works as an online program for generating short-term loans to credit union members. As we've noted, unsecured loans, such as payday loans, are not permissible services for CUSOs under NCUA standards. Remember, however, that some states have their own CUSO regulations. This is the case with QCash. It is a CUSO owned exclusively by a Washington State-chartered credit union, and Washington State law permits credit union investment in CUSOs that provide unsecured loans. QCash can therefore make unsecured short-term loans. In fact, QCash could originate the loans themselves under Washington State law, but for now, the credit union itself typically originates the loans underwritten by QCash.

CUSTOMER BASE

According to NCUA regulations, CUSOs must "primarily" serve credit unions and/or credit union members. The term "primarily" is defined as "more than 50 percent of a business," but the exact definition can be understood in different ways. For instance, in the case of an insurance agency, does it refer to more than 50 percent of the people insured, or more than 50 percent of the number of policies sold? Then again, could it refer to more than 50 percent of gross commissions from the sale and maintenance of policies?

Ultimately, the NCUA determines whether a CUSO is primarily serving credit unions and credit union members by using a factor-based test. They look at the overall business, along with several variables to make a determination. Consider, for example, a situation in which more than 50 percent of a CUSO's customers are credit unions and credit union members, but they represent only 10 percent of gross revenue. This type of issue generally arises in business-to-business relationships in which a CUSO is providing services directly to another financial institution, such as a bank that doesn't have credit union membership. That one client could be generating far more income for the CUSO than all its credit union clientele combined.

It presents an interesting quandary. The CUSO wouldn't want to turn that business away. So it would have to find an artful way of serving that business in some other fashion. It's different in every case, but it's an important consideration when a CUSO is forming. All parties to the CUSO, including service providers or entrepreneurs who are thinking of partnering with credit unions for investment, need to know the implications. They need to understand that the company is primarily designed to focus on serving the credit union industry.

The key for a CUSO is to decide at the beginning which variable makes the most sense to determine whether the CUSO is primarily serving a credit union and/or members. Once a variable is chosen, it shouldn't be changed on a whim just to suit the numbers. It should only change if the business model changes as a whole. For example, a CUSO may start out providing services in one sphere, then branch out to provide additional services in another arena. When that happens, it may be necessary to change the variable used to determine percentages. The CUSO should assess the new business model and determine how the CUSO is primarily serving credit unions and/or members. It's important for a CUSO to have a firm grasp of how to maximize the "primarily serves" requirement in its business model.

The "more than 50 percent rule" does provide some flexibility. However, a CUSO's ability to grow its business can seem limited because CUSOs must primarily serve credit unions and credit union members. For instance, consider a CUSO partnership between a credit union and an entrepreneur who has developed innovative loan origination software. By NCUA regulations, more than 50 percent of the loan origination has to be with credit union members. If a community or commercial bank comes along with an interest in using the service, the CUSO will have to make sure that non-credit union clients don't exceed credit union clients.

On the other hand, "the more than 50 percent rule" does leave room for up to 49 percent of a CUSO's business to be with non-credit unions and/or members. CUSOs therefore open doors of opportunity for credit unions to expand their client base beyond their own membership communities. A credit union, for example, can broaden its market for making mortgage loans beyond its own members by forming a CUSO that also serves non-credit union members.

CUSOs also allow credit unions to use the money of

non-credit union customers and investment partners to help fund credit union services. A credit union can therefore generate capital and reduce expenses by forming a CUSO to serve people and entities outside their field of membership. Without the commercial advantage of a CUSO, a credit union's charter is exclusive to its own membership. By establishing a CUSO, credit unions can widen their field of operations and grow, as long as they meet the "primarily serves" requirement for their customer base.

LEGAL ADMINISTRATIVE REQUIREMENTS

The third pillar of CUSO regulation comprises legal administrative requirements that apply to both federally chartered credit unions and state-chartered credit unions. These requirements relate to the financial health of credit unions that invest in CUSOs. The NCUA is duty bound to ensure the safety and soundness of the insurance fund administered by the NCUA. They want to make certain that investment in CUSOs doesn't hamper the financial well-being of credit union investors.

This area of regulation requires CUSOs to:

- Produce quarterly financial statements
- Keep books and records in accordance with Generally Accepted Accounting Principles (GAAP)

- Obtain annual independent audits by a licensed CPA
- Allow NCUA access to books and records
- Register with the NCUA on an annual basis

NCUA and state regulatory authorities will review the books, records, and internal controls of a CUSO in order to determine whether the company is operating in a safe and sound manner. The reasoning behind these regulations is to protect credit union investment in CUSOs, along with any operational risk.

CUSOs are also annually required to submit information directly to the NCUA. That information includes details such as a listing of credit unions invested in the CUSO, the types of services the CUSO provides, and the financials of the CUSO. If the CUSO is providing lending services, they have to report the total dollar amount of loans they are servicing or holding on their books. If they are providing IT services, they have to provide information about those services.

A credit union that invests in a CUSO must also obtain an attorney opinion letter stating that the credit union's liability is limited to the investment in the CUSO. Limited liability is a legal protection that applies to any investor in a business. It would apply to Warren Buffett and his company, Berkshire Hathaway, investing in Wells Fargo. It's a legal protection that protects Buffett by limiting his liability to only the investment in Wells Fargo as a separate legal entity.

For a credit union, the attorney opinion letter delineates the amount of liability the credit union has in the CUSO as an entity separate from the credit union itself. This limitation of liability is often called the "corporate veil." If a claimant wanted to pierce the corporate veil and sue a credit union for the liabilities of the CUSO, they would have to prove through a factor-based test that the CUSO was not really a separate legal entity but was instead just a division of the credit union.

Determining factors would include questions such as: Are the two entities commingling operating funds? Are the two entities made up of the same management teams? Are the two entities keeping separate books and records? And finally, the most important question: Is the entity being sued adequately capitalized? In other words, does it have enough capital and/or insurance coverage to reasonably cover the foreseeable liabilities against it? In order to invest in a CUSO, a credit union must ensure that these factors are being met, and the attorney opinion letter lays it all out.

NCUA REGULATORY REVIEWS

NCUA auditors don't actually have regulatory authority

over CUSOs. As we've seen, their authority is indirect. Their concern is with credit unions themselves, which includes credit union investment in CUSOs. The only authority the NCUA has regarding CUSOs is to ensure that a credit union's investment and potential operational risks are safe, sound, and protected.

Credit unions want to be sure that an NCUA regulatory review is limited to only the safety and soundness of their CUSO investment. For the most part, NCUA staff spend their time regulating credit unions, and credit unions are very different from CUSOs. Their balance sheets are different, their business model is different—everything is essentially different. However, NCUA staff tend to want to review CUSOs as if they are credit unions. This can create problems and can often lead to NCUA staff asking to review information that is not relevant to the safety and soundness of a credit union's CUSO investment.

I've seen situations where the NCUA has asked CUSOs for all employment agreements and compensation to employees. That doesn't seem appropriate or relevant to the NCUA mission. CUSOs allow access to their books and records only to facilitate assessment of the safety and soundness of credit union investment and possible operational risk. This shouldn't require that CUSOs turns over the keys and say, "Go wherever you want."

Even if a CUSO were to give the NCUA access to information outside the scope of their review, it's not the NCUA's place to comment on those findings. If they see information on executive compensation, for example, they shouldn't be offering an opinion on the CEO's pay. The furthest they should go is in addressing operational or investment risks.

Ultimately, the NCUA is concerned with the safety and soundness of its institutions, which translates as concern for the safety and soundness of CUSO investments. If the NCUA has a problem with a CUSO investment, it can force a credit union to divest from the CUSO, but they would only force a divestiture under extreme circumstances. Divestiture really puts a CUSO in a difficult position when dealing with the NCUA. The NCUA doesn't have regulatory authority over CUSOs, but they can possibly force compliance by threatening to cripple the CUSO's capital structure. A CUSO generally can't fight. They can only agree, because the threat of divestiture is too great. Divestiture is life threatening to a CUSO. As a threat, it's a strong incentive that forces a CUSO to come to some terms with the NCUA and address their concerns.

HANDLING AN EXAMINATION

NCUA auditors have a job to do, but the regulatory examination process can, by definition, be a bit adversarial. I always say that the best institutions are those that establish good relationships with their examiners; they don't try to be sneaky and hide things or give auditors a hard time. It's important to have good rapport so that the examiner feels confident in a CUSO's goodwill and transparency.

One concern with the examination process has been that CUSOs operate in many different industries and services that aren't exclusively related to the traditional scope of credit unions as financial institutions. As stated above, CUSOs have different business models and balance sheets. NCUA examiners who specialize in credit unions may not have the background and experience necessary for reviewing the activities of a CUSO that is, say, a broker-dealer or an insurance agency. One of the issues that arises is that the examiner coming in to audit a CUSO's financial records may not really understand how finances work in that CUSO's specialized industry. This can create problems that add to an adversarial climate. However, a well-run CUSO with good documentation and accurate and complete records will not run into as many problems.

When the NCUA does an audit, they come in-house. They'll arrive at a CUSO's offices and stay a week or two reviewing everything they consider relevant. The process can be intense. To smooth the process, CUSOs need to have all their documentation in place and ready to be reviewed. I recommend keeping everything up to date in a share drive. It doesn't instill confidence to be scrambling around trying to find documentation. It will only raise red flags and make a CUSO appear disorganized. An auditor will only want to dig deeper and find out what else may be wrong.

It's a good idea for a CUSO to have a point person to work with auditors on their review. This staff member should know where everything is, just in case something is missing from the binder or disc. If an auditor asks for something obscure, the point person should be there to find it quickly and easily.

TELL YOUR STORY

I always advise my clients that the best way to handle the examination process is to use it as a teaching opportunity to show an auditor the intrinsic value of their CUSO. It's a chance for a credit union to tell the story of how their CUSO benefits both the credit union and its membership. CUSOs come with advantages of increased services and financial products that substantially improve members' lives. They allow credit unions to compete on equal footing with other financial institutions and expand their vital role in the community.

One of my clients is the CEO of a credit union with many CUSO investments, and he's a veteran of many audits. He told me that anytime an examiner asks him a question about one of his CUSOs, he makes sure to reply with some variation of, "You mean the CUSO that provides X, Y, Z opportunity, or the CUSO that has provided X amount of income or profit for the credit union?" He wants to seize the opportunity to tell his CUSO story and make sure the examiner understands the context of the CUSO, and how the investment has brought greater profitability and opportunity to the credit union.

CUSO stories have the power to change a sterile regulatory process into a human encounter with real communication. Using regulatory audits as educational opportunities serves to defuse the adversarial dynamic by which auditors perceive CUSOs as potential threats to the safety and soundness of credit unions. Instead, an audit can be used as an occasion to change the narrative and shed a positive light on the beneficial role CUSOs play in our communities and in the ever-expanding financial marketplace.

CONCLUSION

WINDOWS OF OPPORTUNITY

In the credit union world, CUSOs are, and will continue to be, a valuable approach to improving income, cutting costs, and providing more and better member services.

SUSTAINABILITY THROUGH CUSOS

As we've seen, the traditional credit union business model is no longer sustainable. In recent times, operating expenses have escalated along with the costs of compliance and technology, while the income yield of credit unions has shrunk. The old model of taking member deposits at a certain interest rate and making loans at a higher interest rate has become obsolete.

The income credit unions receive from interest on loans

is no longer enough to exceed their operating expenses. These changes have threatened the very survival of credit unions in an evolving financial marketplace. At the same time, however, credit unions have continued to be relevant to their communities. Consumers are increasingly attracted to credit unions as nonprofit, member-owned institutions that provide community-based financial services at significantly lower costs and higher levels of service than corporate banks.

To meet growing consumer needs and to not only survive but thrive in the new digital marketplace, credit unions have embraced a new business model of sustainability. They are maximizing efficiencies by joining together in collaborative CUSOs that have the collective ability to expand financial services while lowering costs through economies of scale. Credit unions are cooperating and innovating through CUSOs to generate additional income, tap into greater expertise, reduce spending, and increase profitability.

PARTNERING FOR INNOVATION

Since the advent of the internet and mobile devices, disruptive technologies have altered the banking industry. In the new digital era, the traditional banking model has given way to innovation by tech entrepreneurs who develop innovative applications that bring the convenience of financial services directly to customers.

Credit unions began as disruptors and innovators a century ago. They recognized the problems of communities that needed access to loans but couldn't get them through established banks. In the new digital era, credit unions have gone back to their roots as innovators, partnering in CUSOs with fintech entrepreneurs and service providers to move past old models into the new digital environment. CUSOs and credit unions are using data and predictive analytics to develop financial services streamlined for their members. These new delivery channels are continuing to open doors for credit unions to invest in leading-edge financial products via CUSO partnerships.

Through their collaboration in CUSOs, credit unions are generating growth opportunities in the ever more competitive financial market. CUSOs facilitate opportunities for credit unions to innovate by partnering to develop new technologies, including payment services, lending platforms, remote banking, and online loan application processes. CUSOs are at the forefront of expanding credit union service delivery channels across new digital platforms.

THE CUSO REVOLUTION

Today's youngest cohorts of consumers tend to be community oriented and inspired by activism and volunteerism. They are natural customers for the cooperative, nonprofit tradition of credit unions. These savvy young consumers are also the entrepreneurs and innovators of today and tomorrow and are natural partners in joining with credit unions to innovate through CUSOs.

By continuing to harness the cooperative spirit, CUSOs are positioned on the front lines of the fintech revolution. By partnering to form CUSOs, credit unions are bringing ever more value to their members and communities while driving growth, especially in the sphere of mobile banking applications.

The history and experience of credit unions demonstrate that shared problems lead to shared solutions. Credit unions and their CUSO partners are finding new strategies for solving problems through innovative products and services. In the growing financial services environment, CUSOs have become windows of opportunity.

NEXT STEPS

Now that you know the contours of the CUSO landscape, I invite you to find out more about CUSOs at our website: www.cusolaw.com. We work at the crossroads of credit unions, regulators, and private sector innovation, advising clients on evolving trends and opportunities in the CUSO marketplace.

In addition, the National Association of Credit Union Service Organizations (NACUSO) is at the forefront of the CUSO industry. NACUSO hosts one of the most rewarding conferences of the year dedicated to collaboration, innovation, and enhancing the credit union industry through CUSOs. More information about NACUSO can be found at www.nacuso.org.

ABOUT THE AUTHOR

 **BRIAN LAUER** is a partner at Messick Lauer & Smith P.C. and a thought leader in the creation of forward-thinking strategies that link credit unions with private sector entrepreneurs. As an attorney, he steers clients through the sea of regulations and governance issues that accompany the formation and day-to-day operations of CUSOs and has helped hundreds of credit unions and CUSOs innovate, collaborate, and generate more net income. Brian is a much sought-after speaker and facilitator at conferences, seminars, and planning sessions at the crossroads where financial services and new digital markets intersect. Learn more at his website: www.cusolaw.com.

Made in the USA
Columbia, SC
02 February 2024

31366884R00079